Christian Vision

Belarus Knockin' at the Vatican's Doors

Appeals of the Belarusian Civil Society in the Context of the Political Crisis 2020

Christian Vision

Christian Vision

is a group of priests, theologians and activists from the Orthodox, Roman and Greek Catholic, Anglican and Evangelical churches who gathered in one team and community in September 2020. It monitors and researches the persecution of Christians and Christian communities in Belarus in the context of the political crisis, supports political prisoners and refugees, protests against the violation of the freedom to believe and practice religion, and informs the international Christian community about the situation in Belarus.

belarus2020.churchby.info
christian.vision.by@gmail.com

ISBN 978-1-915601-07-0

Published by Skaryna Press for Christian Vision
skarynapress.com

© Individual authors, texts, 2022
© Hanna and Christian Vision, cover design, 2022

Table of Contents

Introduction 1

Sviatlana Tsikhanouskaya
Fraternal Society: A Vision for a New Belarus.'s letter 5

Rev. Viachaslau Barok
Pope Francis, How to Stop the War in Belarus? How to Stop Evil? 19

Volha Seviarynets
From Mum of Frančišak to Holy Father Francesco 23

Christian Vision
Cover Letter of Volha Seviarynets's Letter to Pope Francis 27

Belarusian Political Prisoners' Wives and Mothers
Letter to Pope Francis 29

Ihar Losik
Letter to Pope Francis 33

Christian Vision
Cover Letter of Ihar Losik's Letter to Pope Francis 35

Christian Vision
Letter to Cardinal Pietro Parolin, the Secretary of State of His Holiness 38

Natallia Vasilevich
The Vatican's Reactions to the Belarusian Crisis 44

Introduction

This book consists of the appeals of Belarusian Christians and participants in the pro-democracy movement in Belarus. They were addressed to the Holy Father Pope Francis and to the Holy See in the context of the political crisis in Belarus, which followed the 2020 presidential elections and continues to this day.

The voices of theologians, politicians, priests, political prisoners and their wives and mothers; voices from behind bars and from exile are present here; voices of despair and hope; intimate and the public; voices full of pain and dignity.

In 2020, a true revolution took place in Belarus, which had been ruled by an authoritarian regime for more than twenty years. This revolution did not produce democratic changes in the political system of the country. However, it led to a change in people's consciousness and the birth of civil society: as if people noticed each other for the first time. They turned to each other, offered to help each other and united to help others. Previously highly atomised and individualised, Belarusian society suddenly became a society of friendship and brotherhood. We felt that we were all brothers and sisters, *fratelli tutti*. The Belarusian protest was completely peaceful and in search of dialogue.

Unfortunately, the authoritarian regime that monopolised power in the country had no other means of interaction with civil society than that of violence, oppression, persecution and disregard for the law. The white flowers of peaceful protesters were met with the black batons of the riot police.

This is the theme taken by the leader of the democratic movement of Belarus **Sviatlana Tsikhanouskaya**'s letter to the Holy Father, *Fraternal Society: A Vision For a New Belarus*, written in November-

December 2020 in response to the encyclical *Fratelli Tutti*. Then, we still felt the aftertaste of an unusual sense of rising spirits and solidarity in our society. However, we could already feel the advance of the machinery of repression. Tsikhanouskaya recognised the description of what was happening to us and around us in the images and ideas of the encyclical. She asked the Holy Father for advice: what should we do to achieve peace and justice in a situation of defeat, where violence and lawlessness prevail?

For two years, Tsikhanouskaya has continued her work as a leader of the pro-democratic movement. She is in exile in Lithuania, unable to return to Belarus where her husband Siarhei is serving an eighteen-year term in prison. Despite all the violence and absurdity happening in Belarus (particularly after the Lukashenko regime involved the country in an aggressive war with the people of Ukraine) and despite limited opportunities to influence the situation, Tsikhanouskaya and her team of politicians, economists, legal experts, human rights advocates and representatives of civil society are making every effort to create the foundations of a new Belarus.

Persecutions affected a large number of people. Even priests were imprisoned. **Fr Viachaslau Barok**, a parish priest in the small town of Rasony and the most popular Catholic blogger in Belarus, was condemned for his Christian position and courage in not remaining silent in the face of lawlessness. He was mockingly accused of 'extremism'. On the eve of his arrest, already knowing that he might end up behind bars, Fr Barok recorded his video appeal to the Holy Father asking him to give attention to Belarus and what was happening there. Six months later, the priest was threatened with arrest again. He was forced to leave the country and is now ministering to Belarusian refugees in Poland, as well as continuing to blog.

The book also contains a letter from **Ihar Losik,** a member of the Catholic faithful and a media expert. He is one of more than two thousand political prisoners in Belarus. He wrote his letter to the Holy Father from behind bars in August 2021. He addressed him as a father begging him to come to his aid, to help stop injustice and lawlessness. Losik was sentenced to fifteen years in prison and is currently serving his term.

Just as this book was about to be sent to print, we learnt that Ihar Losik's wife, Daria, was detained by riot police. She is accused in "assisting extremism", as the authorities interpreted her interview to Belsat, a Poland-based TV channel. Their daughter, Paŭlina, was left to stay with her grandparents, Daria's parents.

The Mothers and wives of political prisoners also wrote letters to Pope Francis. First, a member of the Catholic faithful, Volha Sevyarynets, wrote a letter about her husband **Paval Sieviaryniec**, an Orthodox Christian. Later, the Vyzvalenne 2020 initiative, which united relatives of political prisoners in Belarus and sought their release, turned to the Holy Father telling him about the situation of the most vulnerable prisoners.

Ales Bialiatski, a human rights activist and a prominent figure of the Catholic revival in the 1990s, is among the political prisoners too. He was first imprisoned for four-and-half years in 2011. The then-Nuncio Claudio Gugerotti visited him in prison on behalf of Pope Benedict XVI to give his blessing to the political prisoner. In his book *Prison Notebooks* Bialatski described this meeting:

> *Gudgerotti said: "I will be seeing the Pope in October. What should I tell him?" — Tell him that your visit was the greatest event in my life — the Pope's attention and concern for us. [...] Let's hope that his intercession for political prisoners in Belarus will bear fruit.*

The voice of the Catholic Ales Bialiatski can now be heard throughout the world — together with the Russian organisation Memorial and the Ukrainian Centre for Civil Liberties, he was awarded the Nobel Peace Prize. However, together with his colleagues from the Viasna human rights organisation, he is in prison again — like thousands of other Belarusian political prisoners. His words about the Pope's intercession for Belarusian prisoners of conscience remain as relevant as ever.

Pope Francis is known as someone who reaches for the forgotten, abandoned and rejected. The Pontiff's public rhetoric appeals to human dignity and the protection of those who suffer from injustice and lawlessness in their various manifestations.

The letters collected here have not yet been answered. In the article concluding this book, the moderator of the Christian Vision group, **Natallia Vasilevich**, looks for an answer to why the day has not yet come when Belarusians feel the care of the head of the Catholic Church.

Christian Vision is a group of priests, theologians and activists from the Orthodox, Roman and Greek Catholic, Anglican and Evangelical churches who gathered in one team and community in September 2020. It monitors and researches the persecution of Christians and Christian communities in Belarus in the context of the political crisis, supports political prisoners and refugees, protests against the violation of the freedom to believe and practice religion, and informs the international Christian community about the situation in Belarus. The members of the group pray together and look for ways to restore the rule of law, peace, justice, democracy and respect for human dignity in our country. Since 24 February 2022 when the war in Ukraine started, Christian Vision has organised solidarity campaigns and events in Belarus and abroad.

Christian Vision has repeatedly appealed to the Pope and the Holy See. This book of selected letters and appeals is powerful evidence of Belarusians' strong faith in the current desperate situation. The letters to the Holy Father have already become part of history — a history with an open ending.

Fraternal Society: A Vision for a New Belarus

*Sviatlana Tsikhanouskaya's letter
to the Holy Father Francis, Bishop, and Pope of Rome,
inspired by his encyclical Fratelli Tutti*

Your Holiness,

My letter is a response to the invitation to dialogue to which you call all people of goodwill in your new encyclical, Fratelli Tutti. This address is inspired by your proposed "vision of fraternal society" (§4), in which "by acknowledging the dignity of each human person, we can contribute to the rebirth of a universal aspiration to fraternity" (§8). In this letter, I want to share the dreams of the Belarusian people, which they "dream together" and which are "built together" (§8) — dreams that resonate with the vision of a fraternal society, ways to implement what you discuss in your encyclical. I want to share these dreams, but also the obstacles and difficulties we face along the way. Therefore, my letter also includes many questions.

For decades, Belarusian society has been subject to the worst form of alienation as identified by the encyclical — "feel[ing] uprooted, belonging to no one" (§53). The Belarusian people have survived since ancient times thanks to communal solidarity and self-organisation — one of its forms, *talaka*, was widespread among Belarusians. But having survived centuries of wars, poverty, oppression, repression, and various cataclysms, including the accident at the Chernobyl nuclear power plant, in the mid-1990s the Belarusians chose a government that promised stability and security. As it turned out, this was at the cost of freedom, the right to elect, and independence.

The contemporary state authorities, which operate on the principle of a rigid hierarchy, with power concentrated in the hands of one person, have prevented, in every way, any forms of community expression and solidarity, except that which is authorised from above. Any joint action within associations — whether by non-governmental organisations, religious communities, political parties, or trade unions — has been either banned or tightly controlled and suppressed. The words "democracy, freedom, justice, [and] unity" (§14) and even the very word "people" (§157) have been uttered constantly, but were perceived as empty sounds and demagoguery, because they were used for manipulation, as tools of domination and as justifications for deception, cruelty, and violence.

There has been a complete alienation of the people — who are the source of sovereignty — from the state, from the sphere of decision-making. Those who have tried to say something, to effect change, to offer an alternative, have been subjected to repression: activists, human rights defenders, and politicians have been expelled from universities, dismissed from work, and arrested. In 2010, seven out of ten presidential candidates were detained, some of whom spent months or years in detention. On the one hand, participation in political activities and expressing one's opinion and position could neither influence nor change anything; on the other hand, it was a great risk for oneself, one's family, one's community, one's affairs. Passivity, dictated by powerlessness and fear, has dominated Belarusian society, and it was this that, in the language of the regime, was called "peace." In effect, Belarusian society has gradually become atomized and individualised, "a mere aggregate of individuals" (§157).

As the entire world began to face the coronavirus pandemic, the authorities of Belarus relied on a strategy of ignoring the problem, while doctors, nurses, and other health workers, who put their lives on the line to fight this new sickness, were left completely unprotected. After the Chernobyl accident in the late 1980s, when the Soviet government hid information about the true scale of the disaster and did not take any measures to prevent the effects of radiation on public health and lives; likewise now, during this pandemic, the state authorities have tried to convince people that there is no danger, that the situation is under control, undercounting the figures for the sick and dead, showing a disregard for common sense and for scientific research and, most importantly, displaying disrespect for the life and human dignity of their citizens. In contrast, in the face of this common struggle, Belarusian citizens have united in volunteer initiatives to help medical workers; the people's solidarity with the medics during COVID-19 is a prime example of their sense of humanitarian mission.

In June 2020, hundreds of thousands of residents of Minsk were deprived of access to drinking water for several days when a serious accident occurred and poisonous substances entered the water supply system. A foul-smelling liquid, completely unfit for drinking, flowed from the taps in people's homes. The authorities, instead of organising access to water supplies, denied the very existence of the problem and provided false information about the quality of water. But again, the people themselves united in one large network of mutual aid and transported water from some districts to others.

As a result, on the one hand, public trust in state leadership was completely undermined, and it became obvious that state policy was based on lies and, instead of helping people, public bodies were ready to sacrifice health and lives; on the other hand, a vision of a community, of brotherhood and sisterhood, was born out of mutual assistance and solidarity. The Belarusian people, previously divided, had realised that such a community is a value and an ideal that should not only be pursued in the future but should be implemented now at the level of civil society, despite the obstacles of state institutions and in the face of lawlessness and an authoritarian political regime.

During the recent election campaign, many people had a dream and a vision of a society in which the voice of everyone matters, in which "at the centre of all political, social and economic activity" stands "a human person, who enjoys the highest dignity" (§232), in which conflicts are not hidden and silenced but resolved "through dialogue and open, honest and patient negotiation" (§244), in which there is space for genuine dialogue without "empty diplomacy, dissimulation, double-speak, hidden agendas and good manners that mask reality" (§226).

The desire for unity and solidarity, and the emergence of the self-understanding of a people that has a common goal and desire—despite belonging to different social groups, holding different political beliefs, having different geopolitical orientations, and being motivated by individual interests—have become an incentive for the birth of a political community. Having come together in the face of shared adversity, people have seen clearly the creative power of solidarity and mutual assistance.

The authorities have habitually hindered the process of unification and political activation by throwing leaders in prison on trumped-up charges (my husband, Siarhei Tsikhanouski, was among them), by refusing to acknowledge the signatures collected for nominations for the presidential elections and, by preventing society from forming election commissions and observing the election process. In response to this repression, more and more solidarity and self-organisation has arisen within society itself; overcoming fear and familiar inertia, people have joined a common struggle for honest, fair, and transparent elections.

Believers and clergy of the Roman Catholic Church have been very actively involved in this process: at the initiative of Artiom Tkaczuk, a missionary and social worker, the campaign "A Catholic Does Not Falsify" was launched. Its task was to promote among the broad Catholic community the idea that fair elections are not only a political issue but also a moral one that has to do with faith and living according to one's faith.

Regardless of their political beliefs, people have been united by the desire for fair, transparent, and democratic elections on the road to change, on the road to justice, on the road to the common good. It so happened that I, Sviatlana Tsikhanouskaya, an ordinary Belarusian woman, who, like most Belarusians, was not interested in politics, was passive, and was engaged mainly in the education of my own children, had to take on this mission to become the leader of the movement for fair and just elections. Maryia Kalesnikava and Veronika Tsepkalo shared this fate with me. Each of us embarked on this path not for the sake of power, but to restore belief that the voice of every human being is meaningful, that solidarity can work miracles, that love and non-violence are stronger than violence.

This path has not been easy for us. The Belarusian people have suffered the fate of the traveller from Jerusalem to Jericho in the parable of the Good Samaritan (Luke 10:25-37): "he fell among robbers, who took off his clothes, wounded him and departed, leaving him barely alive." The Belarusian people were robbed: their votes in the elections and their right to know the truth about the election results were stolen. "There is only one way out," Bishop Aleh Butkevich told the Belarusian people: "We need to look for the truth!.. But the truth will not be where there is violence."[1] Metropolitan Tadeusz Kondrusiewicz supported people in their legitimate quest for truth: "People have a right to know the truth, which cannot be sacrificed to someone's political or economic interests."[2]

Driven by the search for the truth about the election results, not allowed to be present at the vote count, people went out to a peaceful demonstration. In response, citizens, journalists, and bystanders were fired at with stun grenades and rubber bullets, beaten, arrested, tortured, and subjected to inhumane and degrading treatment, and their children were forcibly taken away into orphanages. The health of thousands of people was seriously harmed, and some Belarusians even lost their lives — Aliaksandr Taraykouski, Henadz Shutau, Aliaksandr Vikhor, Kanstantsin

---

[1] Выйсце адно — шукаць праўду. Біскуп Віцебскі Алег Буткевіч выступіў са Зваротам з нагоды масавых пратэстаў у краіне. *Catholic. by*, 2020-08-12. Available at: https://catholic.by/3/news/belarus/11996-vyjstse-adno-shukats-pra-du-b-skup-v-tsebsk-aleg-butkev-ch-vystup-sa-zvarotam-z-nagody-masavykh-pratesta-u-kra-ne (in Belarusian)

[2] Зварот арцыбіскупа Тадэвуша Кандрусевіча да дзяржаўных уладаў Рэспублікі Беларусь. *Catholic.by*, 2020-08-14. Available at: https://catholic.by/3/news/belarus/12014-zvarot-artsyb-skupa-tadevusha-kandrusev-cha-da-dzyarzha-nykh-ulada-respubl-k-belarus (in Belarusian)

Shyshmakou, Mikita Kryutsou, and Raman Bandarenka. Belarusians, bloodied, with broken teeth, with torn bellies, with broken arms and legs, wounded, unable to even scream in pain, were thrown onto the floor in prisoner transport vehicles, on the ground in the yards of police stations, and on the concrete floors of prisons, feeling completely helpless.

In response to this horrific violence, women took to the streets of Belarusian cities; then doctors, musicians, athletes, scientists, students, pensioners, and people with disabilities followed. Archbishop Artemy of Hrodna, of the Belarusian Orthodox Church, called the women's protest — in which wives, mothers, and sisters of beaten husbands, sons, brothers came out to the streets with flowers and smiles — a real miracle, the implementation of the spiritual law: "Don't be defeated by evil, but defeat evil with good!" (Romans, 12.21). Thus, love "returned peace and stopped violence" — it became a healing force "from the toxins of evil and aggression"[3]. Petra Bosse-Huber, a bishop of the Evangelical Church in Germany, saw in the brave Belarusian women who follow the path of peace and love and implement the principle of this spiritual law "the image of Mary, protecting and covering with her protecting veil"[4]. The Roman Catholic bishop Yury Kasabutski also compared Belarusian women with Mary, who stood by the cross without fear and looked at the suffering of her Son: "You took the flowers, you came out, you stood, you showed the world, which confused all people… Your smiles — you just amazed everyone; everyone was in shock… You came out and you have started

---

[3] Обращение Архиепископа Артемия Гродненского и Волковысского. Catholic.by, 2020-08-14. Available at:
https://belarus2020.churchby.info/obrashhenie-arxiepiskopa-artemiya-grodnenskogo-i-volkovysskogo/ (in Russian); Öffentlicher Appel von Artemij, Erzbischof von Grodno und Volkovysk, *Church and the Political Crisis in Belarus*, 2020-08-14. Available at:
https://belarus2020.churchby.info/offentlicher-appel-von-artemij-erzbischof-von-grodno-und-volkovysk/ (in German)

[4] Bild der schützenden und schirmenden Maria ist wie ein Vorbild, EKD-Auslandsbischöfin bekundet Solidarität mit Mitgliedern der Arbeitsgruppe „Christliche Vision" des oppositionellen Koordinierungsrates für Belarus. Evangelische Kirche in Deutschland, 2020-10-12. Available at:
https://www.ekd.de/bild-der-schuetzenden-und-schirmenden-maria-ist-wie-ein-vorbild-59577.htm (in German)

defeating evil with good... You may have defeated the devil without knowing it... Our Belarusian girls, women, our daughters, sisters, wives, mothers, grandmothers — you are heroes of our time"[5].

Christian women were also among the first to organise special prayers for Belarus amid a growing wave of violence and lawlessness against peaceful protesters. On August 12, Catholic believer Irena Bernatskaya from the city of Lida began to pray the rosary daily in the form of the Rosary Novena to Our Lady of Pompeii, for peace in Belarus, for which she was subjected to a large fine on October 16. On August 13, several Orthodox women from Minsk initiated ecumenical prayers in the centre of the city, in the square between the Holy Spirit Orthodox Cathedral and the Catholic Arch-Cathedral of the Holy Name of the Blessed Virgin Mary. Orthodox, Catholics, Protestants prayed together and then passed in procession with banners, icons, and Bibles through the streets of the city. A group of women believers in Minsk also goes out every evening to pray the rosary for Belarus and for the return from exile of Archbishop Tadeusz Kondrusiewicz. A young Greek Catholic believer Marysia Bulatouskaya from Viciebsk was fined for being near a peaceful procession and praying. On October 4, an elderly believer from Brest, Elena Gnauk, knelt between protesters and the police, praying for peace, and for this was punished with 18 days in detention, and now faces the threat of criminal prosecution.

Many ministers from different churches did not become like the priest and the Levite in the parable; they did not pass by, afraid to be desecrated by "worldly affairs". Their answer was prayer, mercy, and the raising of their voices against violence and lawlessness.

Two large interfaith prayers were held in Minsk and Hrodna. In Minsk, on the initiative of Archbishop Tadeusz Kondrusiewicz, on August 19, an inter-religious prayer for peace in Belarus took place — it was the Catholic archbishop who initiated such a prayer, attended by priests of the

---

[5] Казань біскупа Юрыя Касабуцкага, Генеральнага вікарыя Мінска-Магілёўскай архідыяцэзіі, *Church and the Political Crisis in Belarus*, 2020-09-05. Available at: https://belarus2020.churchby.info/kazan-biskupa-yuryya-kasabuckaga-generalnaga-vikaryya-minska-magilyoŭskaj-arxidyyacezii-5-09-2020/ (in Belarusian).

Catholic, Orthodox, Protestant churches, as well as Belarusian Jews and Muslims. In Hrodna, at the general initiative of religious organisations of different denominations, on August 16, in the historical city centre, an interfaith prayer procession was organised with posters of spiritual content and against violence, for the peaceful resolution of the political crisis and the release of the innocent people arrested. Clergy and believers of five Christian denominations, as well as representatives of the Jewish community, took to the streets.

Protestants prayed daily in the centre of Minsk and special services were held in many Orthodox, Catholic and Protestant churches. In Hrodna, the Orthodox churches rang their bells every hour. In September, at the initiative of Archbishop Tadeusz Kondrusiewicz, the Roman Catholic Church held a pilgrimage to the statue of the holy Archangel Michael, patron saint of the Roman Catholic Church in Belarus and defeater against evil, with the intention of a speedy resolution of the social and political crisis. Under Pavel, the Orthodox Metropolitan of Minsk, who followed the initiative of the faithful women who began prayers near the cathedral, prayers for Belarus became a daily occurrence. The new leader of the Belarusian Orthodox Church, Metropolitan Veniamin of Minsk, who succeeded Metropolitan Pavel, called twice for the congregation to fast for several days. Prayers and processions were held in many communities throughout Belarus, despite the fact that even prayers for Belarus became dangerous: in Vaŭkavysk, about fifteen participants in prayer for Belarus, which were held in the Orthodox Church of Saints Methodius and Cyril, Equal to the Apostles, were detained.

Priests also showed mercy and expressed solidarity with suffering. From the first days of the protests, the Greek Catholic priest Ihar Kandratsieu joined the protesters in Brest with prayers and words of support, spending days in the streets of the city and under the walls of the local prison, seeking the release of the beaten detainees. For this, he was pressured and threatened with the de-registration of his community. Orthodox, Catholic, and Protestant priests also met by the walls of detention centres, where detainees and those arrested were held, while in the tent camp of volunteers near the prison of Akrescina there was a prayer corner. Orthodox and Catholic priests in Hrodna and Minsk tried to pass on water, food, basic necessities, and hygiene products to the prisoners. Priests came to court — in Vaŭkavysk, Orthodox priests came from different cities of Belarus to support their colleague, priest Alexander Bogdan, who was tried twice. Priests of four Christian denominations came to Hrodna for the trial of the renowned surgeon, believer Alexander Tsylindz.

Some priests also went out to openly protest against the violence and lawlessness committed. On August 13, Orthodox priest Vladimir Drobyshevski took to the streets of the city of Homieĺ with a poster "Stop the violence". In September, he was convicted twice in succession and held in custody for 25 days. On the very first evening after the elections on August 9, two Roman Catholic Priests of the Sacred Heart of Jesus were jailed — Eduard Sinkevich (10 days) and Alexander Fedotov (8 days). In different cities, priests stood in chains of solidarity and supported peaceful people, and in Lida, Orthodox priests treated women with ice cream. Many opened the doors of Orthodox and Catholic churches so that peaceful protesters could escape from unjust violence and brutality by the police, and were coming out of the churches to talk to the police (in Żodzina, Lida, Hrodna and Minsk) — but this did not always help. Thus, on August 26, the police blocked peaceful protesters and journalists in the Red Church of St. Simeon and Elena in Minsk, and on September 11, several women of faith were brutally detained at the entrance to the church.

In addition, priests posted on social networks and blogs, delivered sermons, spoke in the media, wrote poems, but — most importantly — listened to numerous stories of violence and torture, held people by the hand, hugged them by the shoulders, wiped away tears, cried with those crying, comforted those who grieved, prayed for those who suffered from bodily and mental wounds, provided material assistance, and stood by their parishioners. Twice a week in his video blog on YouTube Viachaslau Barok, a Roman Catholic priest from a small town of Rasony, offered reflections on the encyclical *Fratelli Tutti* and applying the social doctrine of the Church to our daily life. On 12 November 2020, the local

Investigative Committee department summoned the priest for interrogation. He is currently facing a criminal prosecution.[6]

In their official statements, the Belarusian churches called for dialogue and peace. On August 16, the Synod of the Belarusian Orthodox Church declared the need to end the violence.[7] In August, fifty Protestant pastors wrote to the people of Belarus.[8] This attempt to participate in a peaceful resolution of the crisis is commendable. The main generator of dialogue, who in various ways tried to find a "architecture of peace" (§231) that could work, was the Metropolitan Tadeusz Kondrusiewicz.

He was the very first to speak up, on August 11, declaring the need for dialogue[9] and a few days later calling on the authorities to "start a constructive dialogue with society, stop the violence, and release all innocent civilians detained at peaceful rallies"[10]. On August 21, Metropolitan Kondrusiewicz even initiated a meeting with Interior Minister Yuri Karayev to personally raise questions about the unrestricted violence used by police officers against civilians. Metropolitan Kondrusiewicz tried using all possible means to find ways to resolve the situation and relieve tension — through prayer, interfaith cooperation,

---

[6] 15 November 2022, Fr Viachaslau Barok issued his appeal addressing Your Holiness. Available from: https://www.youtube.com/watch?v=CajfYcdOQzg (in Belarusian with Russian, English, German, Polish subtitles).

[7] Обращение Синода Белорусской Православной Церкви к народу Республики Беларусь о прекращении народного противостояния. *Официальный портал Белорусской православной Церкви*, 2020-08-15. Available from: http://www.church.by/news/obrashenie-sinoda-belorusskoj-pravoslavnoj-cerkvi-k-narodu-respubliki-belarus-o-prekrashenii-narodnogo-protivostojanija (in Russian).

[8] Открытое обращение Евангельских протестантских церквей к народу Беларуси, 2020-08-20. Available from: https://belarus2020.churchby.info/otkrytoe-obrashhenie-evangelskix-protestantskix-cerkvej-k-narodu-belarusi (in Russian).

[9] Зварот арцыбіскупа Тадэвуша Кандрусевіча ў сувязі са складанай грамадска-палітычнай сітуацыяй у Беларусі, 2020-08-11. Available from: https://catholic.by/3/news/belarus/11991-zvarot-artsyb-skupa-tadevusha-kandrusev-cha-suvyaz-sa-skladanaj-gramadska-pal-tychnaj-s-tuatsyyaj-u-belarus (in Belarusian).

[10] Зварот арцыбіскупа Тадэвуша Кандрусевіча да дзяржаўных уладаў Рэспублікі Беларусь, 2020-08-14. Available from: https://catholic.by/3/news/belarus/12014-zvarot-artsyb-skupa-tadevusha-kandrusev-cha-da-dzyarzha-nykh-ulada-respubl-k-belarus (in Belarusian).

calls for dialogue, and appeals to the state authorities. Tadeusz Kondrusiewicz became an example of a religious leader among those who are "called to be true 'people of dialogue'" (§284). He became an example of an "authentic mediator" who, by raising his voice about the need for dialogue, "spends himself generously until he is consumed, knowing that the only gain is peace" (§284). He represented a church, "that serves, that leaves home and goes forth from its places of worship, goes forth from its sacristies, in order to accompany life, to sustain hope, to be the sign of unity... to build bridges, to break down walls, to sow seeds of reconciliation" (§276). However, to his words about peace, dialogue, mercy, truth, and non-violence, the authorities responded with repression, saying that it is not the church's business to "interfere in politics"[11] — and the Metropolitan found himself in exile, in which he has been for more than two months.

We, the Belarusian people, want dialogue. For our part, we have created a dialogue platform — the Coordinating Council — which included authoritative representatives from politics, science, culture, business, media, sports, and charity, and religious communities were also invited to active participation. The Coordinating Council has a Christian Vision Working Group, which was created by theologians, priests, and active believers of the Orthodox, Catholic, and Protestant churches. It is an example of ecumenical cooperation and dialogue for the common good.

We seek truth and justice, an end to violence and the release of political prisoners, and new, fair, just, and democratic elections. This is not a struggle of political ideologies and clans, parties and social groups. It is a desire to live in a society built on a solid foundation of truth, justice, love, and dialogue. It is not only our right, but now it is our duty, because peace and forgiveness do not, as you yourself say, "forbid" justice to those who are subjected to injustice, does not "forbid" the defence of their rights, "but actually demand it" (§241).

---

[11] Лукашенко: церкви, костелы — не для политики. *БелТА*, 2020-08-22. Available from: https://www.belta.by/president/view/lukashenko-hramy-kostely-ne-dlja-politiki-403780-2020 (in Russian).

But how should we build this dialogue? How can we demand justice if one party — the one that has weapons and power — is not going to return stolen votes or restore justice or stop violence and repression, but proposes only to "move on", "to turn the page", to accept injustice, saying that it is necessary "to look to the future" (§249)?

We also look to the future and dream of the future, but our vision of the new Belarus is a vision of a fraternal community of solidarity and mutual assistance, which we have experienced ourselves and continue to experience now, and which feeds our hopes for the future.

Despite all the repression and violence, the protest continues to be peaceful; moreover, the spirit of mutual help and solidarity grows in it, as leaven in dough. Our eyes have already seen, our ears have already heard, our hands have already touched, our mouths have already had a foretaste of the society that Belarus could be. We know what we want and what we aspire to — a new brotherly, united, inclusive Belarus, one that already exists in city quarters in which neighbours did not know each other yesterday and today gather to drink tea, treat each other with cake, sing and dance together. It exists in businesses: in private medical centres that provide free diagnosis and treatment for victims of police violence, in flower shops that give flowers to women, in confectionery shops that treat people with candy, and in service stations that repair cars for free. This society shows itself in a street choir of pensioners singing the spiritual anthem *Mahutny Boża* (Almighty God), in the lectures of philosophers in the playground, in the sincere prayer of Orthodox and Protestant believers at the Red Church in support of the exiled Catholic archbishop. It is being born in workers' teams, in university classrooms, in art studios, in prayer circles, in village clubs. The faces and actions of the Belarusian peaceful movement are so different, "involving millions of actions, great and small, creatively intertwined like words in a poem" (§169), but we all live with one dream and one vision—the fraternal society.

Three months after the beginning of the protests, another tragedy happened. On November 11, a 31-year-old artist and activist, Raman Bandarenka, was kidnapped by unknown persons in the courtyard of his own house, after which he ended up at the police station. From there, he was taken to hospital in a coma after being severely beaten. The next day, he died. The death of Raman shocked the entire Belarusian society. Believers of different traditions — Orthodox, Roman and Greek Catholics, Protestants and others — gathered to pray for the repose of his soul. At the mass in the Minsk Catholic Cathedral , there were no fewer people than at Christmas and Easter. On Sunday, November 15, people from all over Minsk came to the courtyard where Raman lived to honour his memory. However, the authorities reacted extremely harshly — more than a thousand participants in the mourning procession were arrested and the spontaneous memorial of candles and flowers was destroyed. There are more and more victims, but the state does not see the problem; not a single criminal case has been initiated against those responsible for these atrocities. Instead, the Prosecutor's Office has punished the Vicar Bishop Yury Kasabutski and Father Sergiy Lepin, the press secretary of the Belarusian Orthodox Church, with a warning for publicly condemning the destruction of his memorial. The death of Raman, as well as the suffering of all the people, does not let us stop — but it makes us look for answers to our questions...

How much longer do we have to go down this path? How many more will be arrested, fired from their workplaces, beaten and expelled from the country, before our voice is heard by the authorities? Who will help us stand up and heal our wounds? Who will help us restore justice? When will Metropolitan Tadeusz Kondrusiewicz, who tried to be the voice of the Church and the voice of the people, return to Belarus? Will the voice of the Church and the voice of the people be able to break through the armoured windows of cars, through the shields of the police, through the disabled Internet? What prophetic word has the power to tear down these walls and build bridges?

On behalf of Belarusian people, we ask for Your holy prayers and Your genuine word of truth and justice, which will be a blessing for all of us.

Sviatlana Tsikhanouskaya,
Leader of Democratic Belarus
4 December 2020

Rev. Viachaslau Barok is a well-known Roman Catholic priest, rector of the church of St Josaphat Kuntsevich in Rasony, video blogger. On his YouTube channel over the past year, he has been reviewing the social teaching of the Catholic Church and the events taking place in Belarus from the perspective of this teaching. On November 12, he was summoned to the Investigative Committee "as a witness" in an unknown criminal case, but it was really about his YouTube channel and speeches. He is a member of the Christian Vision group of the Coordinating Council. On 15 November 2020 a Belarusian Catholic priest addressed Pope Francis in his video.

Pope Francis,
How to Stop the War in Belarus?
How to Stop Evil?

Address to Pope Francis by
Rev. Viachaslau Barok[1]

Dear friends, please let me address not you, but Pope Francis today.

Our lives are short; we should not postpone what our hearts desire. While I am still free, though the Investigative Committee is ploughing through all that I preach, I would like to express to you, my friends, my deep gratitude. Then I would like to address the Pope.

I am aware that I am only one of 1,330,000,000 Catholics around the world and one of over 400,000 priests. I understand well that for certain good reasons Belarus is not the Vatican's primary concern. All this suggests that my words have hardly any chance of reaching the Holy See rather than being lost among the thousands of more important concerns.

Still, I would rather try than regret later that I failed to do what was in my power.

Dear Pope Francis, I am asking you to hear not me, but the Belarusian people. It so happened that the authorities of the country have started a war with its own people.

Indeed: a war. Our peace crashed when the elections were rigged, truth was laughed at and justice – stomped upon. The state justice has started judging and convicting not criminals, but their victims. Prisons are full now of victims of violence, not of those who beat them.

Why did it happen?

---

[1] https://belarus2020.churchby.info/pope-francis-how-to-stop-the-war-in-belarus/; https://www.youtube.com/watch?v=jOV4AVkGAVc

It is quite simple: our voices got stolen. We were deprived of free choice. Even God does not take this freedom away, but we were deprived of it. Those who disagreed with this injustice, are now thrown into prisons, fired from work, expelled from universities, beaten, tortured, denigrated and killed.

Nobody knows better than you do how everything turns upside down when a military junta takes power in a country. No doubt, the experience of your motherland, Argentina, with its Dirty War of 1976-83 when nearly 100,000 people suffered badly, allows you to understand our situation very well.

In Belarus, over 26,000 people have already been detained, there are over 100 political prisoners, thousands have been crippled and six – killed. Sure, fewer than during the Dirty War, however the Belarusian law enforcing agencies have not stopped their lawless violence yet. This is after only 100 days of peaceful protests.

Raman Bandarenka died 12 November 2020. In fact, it was a murder. Thugs took him away from Plošča Pieramenaŭ (Square of Changes). This is a usual way for Belarusian law enforcing agencies to commit their crimes: without uniforms or identity signs, but with weapons in their hands and balaclavas on their faces. Raman was killed for his stance on decency and solidarity, for the Belarusian flag symbolising Christ, for belief that goodness will conquer evil. This tragic death of a 31-year old artist shook Belarus. Only those who lost their human sensibilities could have stayed indifferent.

Every Belarusian understands now that unless people fighting for the rule of law overcome lawlessness, a humanitarian catastrophe in the country is inevitable. This war will destroy the nation, the country and the humanity of the people.

The aim of my appeal is to find an answer to the question: what shall we do to bring peace to Belarus? How to stop this war?

I have read your Encyclical, Fratelli Tutti, several times. I explained to others how relevant your message was for Belarus. However, I cannot find an answer to my own question of how it is possible to have a dialogue with those who do not want a dialogue. How is the "architecture of peace" possible without dialogue? Our Metropolitan Tadeusz Kondrusiewicz was expelled from the country as soon as he raised a question of a dialogue.

I am losing faith that those who have had a taste of human blood can come to their senses and start talking.

At the same time, the one who proclaimed that "today is not the right time to observe laws" happily met with your envoy to Belarus, Archbishop Ante Jozić. The regime propaganda happily spread the image of the Nuncio and the person who publicly confessed to ordering the murder of innocent citizens drinking champagne together. This was too much for Belarusians.

In my videos, I tried to explain this event without blaming the policy the Vatican had chosen. Thank you for your care and thoughts about us. However, everyone can see that by calling you "the best Pope", Lukashenko only seeks to hide behind the authority of St Peter's successor. Not behind Cardinal Jorge Bergoglio, but behind Christ's Apostle. He pretends that the Pontiff himself has given him a dispensation for further crimes.

I know definitely that it is not true. So, dear Papa, here is my question: how do we stop this evil in our country?

As someone who opposes lies and violence and, consequently, is against fascism, communism and all the ideologies built on those teachings, I had to explain to law enforcement why I was taking a stance against this evil.

The Investigative Committee summoned for an interview not the famous artist Tsesler, but a priest from the most remote corner of Belarus, because I had posted on social media Tsesler's work "Stop Lukashism", which reflects on the evil of the Belarusian authoritarian regime and its roots in the unrepented crimes of Soviet communism.

Of all this, I am guilty only of preaching the teaching of the Church. I cannot help it.

Dear Papa, in the Encyclical, you said that each of us should discern our roles in the parable of the Samaritan ... I have found mine: having no other options, I lay down next to the beaten and offended man. This is how I see Belarus today, its awakened people.

Dear Papa, tell me, how do you see your role when talking about Belarus? Using the terms from the parable, I understand that the bandits are still on the road and they still beat people. Because of this, there is no way for you to visit our country. Still, how do you see yourself, what is your role?

No doubts, your answer, dear Papa, will help Belarus. Our people have no claims and demands on others. We want only truth, justice, freedom and peace. Is this not what God wants?

Thank you, Pope Francis, for fulfilling your Shepherd's ministry to us and teaching us.

15 November 2020

From Mum of Francišak to Holy Father Francesco

Letter of Volha Seviarynets to Pope Francis

Your Holiness, much-esteemed Pope Francis,

I would not dare to write to you if it were not for the extreme circumstances my dear Belarus and my family have found themselves in. I am turning to you to tell the story of a little boy, Francišak, and his dad.

We live in the Belarusian capital, Minsk. When my husband and I learned that we were expecting a child, the country was celebrating the 500th anniversary of the first Belarusian Bible published by Francis Skaryna. We decided to name our boy in his honour and in your honour — Francišak. He is now three years old. He has been growing up without his dad for more than a year.

This is how long his dad, Paval Sieviaryniec, has been imprisoned for. Paval is a sincere believer, a Christian, a writer. He is among those who revived the legendary party of 1920-30s, the party of Belarusian Christian Democracy. All his work, writings and family life are underpinned with Christian values. His biggest dream is Belarus believing in God. He has committed to this dream without sparing himself.

Since 1994, during the long dictatorship years in Belarus, Paval has spent nearly eight years in jails and in places of penal work following false accusations and unjust sentences. Last year, he was kept in solitary confinement — a small room without windows and personal belongings — for 70 days as an arbitrary punishment. Even the Bible was taken away from him! He did not have a blanket or mattress for sleeping. He used a bottle of water instead of a pillow. For the whole summer, he was deprived of walks and a shower. He could only walk and pray in this inhumane solitary confinement.

At the latest unjust trial, Paval chose to remain silent. He explained his decision by the example of Christ who silently faced unjust accusations. The secret court ignored the fact that Paval's actions were absolutely peaceful and in accordance with the rights provided by the Belarusian Constitution. It sentenced him to seven years of strict regime jail.

There are hundreds of people and stories like mine in Belarus today. Dads, mums with many children, sick people and even children remain in prisons. Their only crime was the desire to live in a free country. They are desperately craving for truth and justice. Each of them carries a cross for Belarus.

Paval is convinced that in today's Belarus everything depends on the Church — whether it will raise its voice for the truth or will continue to live in lies and fear, turning a blind eye to the suffering of people.

Our long-awaited son, Francišak, is growing up without a father. This year, he has learned to speak and can pray the Our Father. He also sings, his favourite song is *I Am Not Afraid, My God Is with Me*. From

prison, Paval sends drawings and letters to Frančišak. He asks him to listen to his mum and pray to God.

Only recently, after a year of Paval's arrest, Frančišak and I were allowed to visit him in a jail. We talked to Paval through the glass. We laughed and prayed together. Frančišak begged his dad to go out with him to play, but Paval was not permitted to do it, although he was guilty of nothing.

Paval is a wonderful father and a beloved husband. I tell my son that his dad is a hero. Frančišak and I love Paval and miss him. I am very afraid that he may never return to us from his Belarusian jail.

We ask you to remember and pray for our family: for Paval and little Frančišak, as well as for all the imprisoned and tortured Belarusians.

We ask you to pray for our country, Belarus. Many of us dream of living in a society rooted in Christian values and truth. Many have done a lot to make this happen one day.

Remember us in prayer.
Long live Belarus! May God be with us!

14 June 2021

Paval Sieviaryniec's hand-drawn St Valentine card for his wife, Volha

Christian Vision's Cover Letter of Volha Seviarynets's Letter to Pope Francis

Holy Father Francis,

We are writing to Your Holiness from Belarus, a country experiencing deep political crisis, violence and lawlessness. We are the Christian Vision group of the Coordination Council for Belarus. It unites clergy, theologians and lay activists of the Orthodox, Catholic and Protestant Churches, and has a profound ecumenical character. The group provides a theological vision for the democratic movement of Belarus based on the Christian social ethos. It serves as a platform for dialogue between the society and Churches on the issues of democratic transition and fostering justice, peace, freedom and solidarity. One of our activities is spiritual and pastoral help to political prisoners — there are nearly 500 of them in Belarus right now — and their families.

Half a year ago Sviatlana Tsikhnanouskaya, the democratic leader of Belarus, addressed Your Holiness in response to your beautiful Encyclical, *Fratelli Tutti*. She was the first political leader in the world to accept your invitation to reflect on peace, justice and solidarity in the community based on brotherhood. Tsikhanouskaya was so eager to address Your Holiness, because for Belarusians nowadays justice, peace, freedom and solidarity are not abstract concepts for dispassionate reflection. Quite the opposite: they are urgent necessities we are striving towards. Sviatlana Tsikhanouskaya is the wife of a political prisoner, Siarhei Tsikhanouski. She became the leader of the Belarusian democratic movement by chance — or, more likely, by Providence — never wanting to be a politician. She accepted her mission for the sake of others. Tsikhanouskaya was the democratic movement's candidate at the presidential elections in August 2020. She received the majority of the votes. The political regime of Alexander Lukashenko which has held power for 27 years refused to recognize her victory and forced her to exile. An unprecedented (for Belarus) tsunami of repression was launched: more than 35,000 people have been detained, almost 500 people have been recognised as political prisoners by the coalition of human rights organisations. At least 15 people have died in these tragic events so far.

We would like to share with Your Holiness a letter. It is not a theological reflection, rather the living story of another political prisoner's wife. Volha Seviaryniec's husband, Paval, is in jail right now. She is taking care of their son, who is your namesake, Francišak. We also would like to add a few details to Volha's story shared with Your Holiness.

Volha is a Roman Catholic, her husband, Paval Sieviaryniec, is an Orthodox Christian. Both are known for their dignified Christian life and dedication to each other, to their homeland, to justice and to Christ. Francišak is their second and the only living child. Their first-born son, Janka, died only a few days after his birth (he was baptised). Janka's severe genetic condition was diagnosed early in Volha's pregnancy. Doctors considered it to be incompatible with postnatal life and suggested an abortion. Volha and Paval put their trust into God and Divine Providence: they categorically rejected the termination and went together through the joy of Jan's birth and the sorrow of his early death. These two Christian spouses have lived through an unspeakable tragedy with a firm belief that every tiny life matters.

Together with the letter, we are enclosing a photograph of Paval, Volha and Francišak taken before Paval's arrest. Also a copy of Paval's hand-made postcard sent from the jail to his beloved wife for St Valentine's: a heart filled with Francišak and Janka, with a church tower, book pages, a cross, flag and the wedding ring in the middle — all that symbolises love means to him.

Please, remember this family in Your holy prayers, together with all the suffering people of Belarus.

Sincerely,

Christian Vision Group
of the Coordination Council
15 June 2021

Letter to Pope Francis by Belarusian Political Prisoners' Wives and Mothers

Your Holiness!

We relatives of political prisoners in Belarus, who have united in the civil initiative Vyzvalennie [Liberation] 2020, are appealing to you.

We were forced to turn to you by the situation in our beloved Belarus, the monstrous violence and injustice that is happening in relation to the citizens of our country, to our loved ones.

Thousands of citizens have ended up in prison in Belarus just because they defended their right to live in a democratic free country and opposed the violence and crimes of the regime. Minors, mothers with many children, and seriously ill people were imprisoned.

Our loved ones are kept behind bars, they are tortured and deprived of the most necessary things. They are held in inhumane conditions, remain without medical care in the midst of a pandemic, and are deprived of their last connection with the world — letters. Our hearts are breaking, but we are not able to help them.

Among political prisoners there are people whose lives are in danger at the moment due to health problems. We know only a fraction of such cases, but they are monstrous. We have included only a few of them in the attachment to the letter.

Ksenia Lutskina, Aliaksei Ramanau, Uladzimir Malachousky, Ryhor Kondruseu, Galina Derbysh, Andrey Voinich, Mikita Zalatarou, Dzmitry Gopta, Antanina Kanavalava, Aliaksei Gubich, Uladzimir Gundar, Andrey Skurko, Volha Klaskouskaya, Palina Sharenda-Panasyuk, Raman Bahnavets, Siarhei Veraschahin, Taciana Lasitsa, Dzianis Ivashyn, Vyachaslau Ragaschchuk, Siarhei Monich, Arciom Bayarsky — we ask for your help for these people. Your authority, the authority of the Catholic Church, can help in their liberation and save their lives.

Our families have been separated for over a year. We cannot spend the brightest holidays — Christmas and Easter — with our dear ones, we cannot hug them on their birthday. They do not see how their children are growing.

In one of your messages, you said: "To be free is a challenge, a constant challenge: it fascinates, captivates, gives courage, encourages to dream, inspires hope, leads to good, gives faith in the future; it is stronger than any slavery. The world needs free people!"

Our relatives remain free-spirited, even while in prison. These are the people the world needs. However, now Belarusian political prisoners, more than ever, need the support of the world.

The Catholic Church has always supported the Belarusian people in their striving for freedom and truth, the doors of the Church have always been open for those seeking justice and peace. We hope for your support now.

Your Holiness!

We, relatives of Belarusian political prisoners, ask you to pray for them and raise your voice against the lawlessness that is happening in Belarus. Help save our loved ones!

We ask you, pray for Belarus!

With deepest respect,
On behalf of the civil initiative
Vyzvalennie 2020,
Coordinators:

Maryna Adamovich
Volha Sevyarynets
Valiantsina Alinevich
Kaciaryna Afnagel
Daria Losik

Annex:

Prisoners in need of urgent qualified medical care

Ksenia Lutskina suffers from bronchial asthma and brain cavernoma; her condition deteriorated sharply during her imprisonment.

Aliaksei Ramanau is 2nd stage disabled owing to cancer. His health deteriorated rapidly in the colony.

Uladzimir Malakhouski, **Ryhor Kondruseu**, and **Halina Dzerbysh** also suffer from oncological diseases and are in need of urgent treatment.

Andrei Voinich has severe liver disease and needs a liver transplant; he is imprisoned already for one year.

Dzmitry Hopta, who has a mental illness, was sentenced to 2 years in prison.

Antanina Kanavalava and **Aliaksei Hubich** have severe eye diseases and might go completely blind without immediate surgical treatment.

Ihar Losik's Letter to Pope Francis

Your Holiness,

My name is **Ihar Losik**. I work for the Belarusian programmes of Radio Liberty/Free Europe. I am a Catholic, the father of a beautiful little girl **Paŭlina**. Sadly, she has been growing up without her dad for more than a year. I have not seen my daughter for more than a year either. I did not hear her first words, nor did I see her first drawings. I am very anxious that she will forget me or even forget the word 'dad'.

Why did this happen? Why has this been going on for over a year? I do not have the answer, nor do I know why more than 600 others are currently suffering in the same way, and thousands more are in real danger. Some will never see their fathers and sons, because they are no longer alive.

I will not be describing the situation in my Belarus. You are probably aware of everything that is happening, especially after Archbishop Tadeusz Kondrusiewicz was not allowed back into the country just because he had a kind heart and could not ignore injustice and violence. Nor will I be explaining the details of my unlawful and absurd criminal prosecution. I just want to tell that many, countless people who found themselves in the same situation are so desperate that the only resolution to everything happening to them, to the suffering from never-ending mental and physical pressure and torture they see in a suicide.

It is hard for me to admit, but I have also been brought to the point where I will just think for days on how to leave this world and stop suffering. I could never imagine that for many months I would be falling asleep and waking up with this thought in the middle of the night.

At first, I tried to prove my innocence by all legal means. Later, out of desperation I went on a **hunger strike for 42 days**. My wife joined my hunger strike too. Every day for two months now she has been standing under the prison walls while I was tried behind closed doors. Threats were made to my family, my two-year-old daughter – these people hold nothing sacred. They just decided to finish me off. They left me no other option but to prove my innocence posthumously. I tried to cut open my veins – fifteen years in prison for nothing, without seeing my daughter is worse than death.

I am not asking you to advocate for me. I am asking to stand up for good, truth and justice, for thousands of Belarusians who have despaired in the same and even worse situations. I am asking Your Holiness to call on these terrible people who do not care about the lives of others, of hundreds of grief-stricken families, to stop.

Maybe I am too naive, and this letter will never reach you. Nevertheless, I am writing it completely sincerely and from the bottom of my heart. I believe that I am writing it for a reason. I really want to believe that God has not abandoned us, that this senseless cruelty will stop, that no one else will die and everyone will return to their families.

With faith and hope, I am asking Your Holiness for blessing, in the name of the Father, and the Son and the Holy Spirit. Amen.

August 2021,
Homieĺ pre-trial detention
centre no. 3

Christian Vision's Cover Letter of Ihar Losik's Letter to Pope Francis

Holy Father Francis,

Today, we are writing to you to bring to Your Holiness's attention the suffering of a political prisoner, the faithful Catholic Ihar Losik. In August 2021 he posted a letter to the Holy See from a pre-trial detention centre where he has already spent **435 days**. We are forwarding an English translation of the original letter a copy of which has been provided by Ihar's wife, **Daria Losik**. In addressing Your Holiness Ihar conveys his fear that his message may never reach You. Therefore we would like to act as pigeon-post to ensure that Ihar's passionate call to Your Holiness has been delivered and heard. With the letter, we enclose pictures of Ihar and his little daughter, **Paŭlina**, who is growing up without her dad, and is able to communicate with him only through her drawings.

It's the second time that we, members of the Christian Vision group of the Coordination Council for Belarus, are writing to You, Holy Father. On 15 June 2021, we shared with Your Holiness a letter from Volha Seviarynets, a political prisoner's wife. Her husband **Paval Sieviaryniec**, is still in jail and unable to give a hand in raising their son who is your namesake, **Francišak**. Our homeland, Belarus, is still in a deep political crisis. It is drowning in violence and lawlessness. Since our last letter to Your Holiness, the number of political prisoners has increased from 500 to nearly 700.

Being a member of the Catholic faithful, **Ihar Losik** sees the last resort for justice and freedom in the Holy Father of the Catholic Church, a world leader of Christians. He desires this justice and freedom not only for himself but for the whole Belarusian people deprived of security and truth. He feels desperate, just as many Belarusians do right now, but he puts his hope in Your compassion and Your Holiness's mission — entrusted to Your power as a Bishop of Rome by Christ Himself — to proclaim justice, peace and the dignity of every human being, and to act so that they prevail in the world.

Ihar's absurd criminal case is bundled together with the one of **Siarhei Tsikhanouski**. His wife, **Sviatlana Tsikhanouskaya**, became a leader of the democratic movement of Belarus and, in all probability, was elected president by the citizens of Belarus in August 2020. In this capacity, she also made history by becoming the first political leader in the world to respond to your profoundly hope-filled Encyclical *Fratelli Tutti*. Though not a theologian, Tsikhanouskaya followed in a heartfelt theological manner your reflection about peace, justice and solidarity for a community based on brotherhood — for Belarus. Justice, peace, freedom and solidarity are far from abstract concepts for our compatriots. They are, rather, an urgent necessity felt throughout the country. This common hunger for truth and justice, shared passion and compassion make us all brothers and sisters and foster parents our community.

Our Christian Vision group has a profound ecumenical character. It has been established in order to offer spiritual and pastoral help to political prisoners, their families, and persecuted individuals and groups. We — Catholic, Orthodox and Protestant clergy, theologians and lay activists — are searching for a theological vision based on the Christian social ethos for the democratic movement in Belarus. We aim to offer a platform for dialogue between our society and the Churches on a democratic transition which fosters justice, peace, freedom and solidarity.

Holy Father, our hearts burn when we read Ihar Losik's letter which is full of despair. We plead to You to help us to turn this despair into hope — just what you so beautifully manage to do in Your pontifical service to the marginalised and oppressed. We plead to You to raise Your apostolic voice to those who are in power to reinstate the rule of law and to start a dialogue for a peaceful and nonviolent resolution of the political crisis in Belarus. We plead for Your prayer to God for all the victims of injustice and persecution in our country, especially for the families already known to You: Ihar, Daria and Paŭlina Losik; Paval, Volha and Francišak Sieviaryniec, as well as for the soul of their firstborn son, Janka.

    Sincerely,

Christian Vision Group
of the Coordination Council
3 September 2021

Letter to Cardinal Pietro Parolin, the Secretary of State of His Holiness

Your Eminence,

The Christian Vision Group of the Coordination Council of Belarus cordially welcomes your letter addressed to us on 26 May 2021, in which You affirmed your attention to the situation in Belarus and assured us of the commitment of the Holy See to democratic and peaceful solutions in response to the legitimate requests of the Belarusian people. Today, on the Feast of the Sacred Heart of Jesus, this commitment was also officially and publicly voiced on behalf of the Apostolic See by the Director of its Press Office, **Mr. Matteo Bruni**.

As Your Eminence and the Apostolic See knows, Christian Vision — a group uniting priests, theologians and lay activists of the Orthodox, Catholic and Protestant Churches concerned with the ongoing political crisis — longs for democratic and peaceful solutions based on respecting the human dignity of every person, with solidarity and justice. Because of this commitment to a peaceful, democratic, lawful approach, however, the Belarusian people have had to pay a very high price — the price of blood, wounds, traumas, tears, imprisonment, exile, insecurity, injustice and, finally, the price of time. The Belarusian people have chosen a noble path of non-violence over violence, dialogue over revolution, new fair elections in pursuit of legitimate demands — over forceful seizure of power. We are very strong, but also very vulnerable in the face of the machinery of repressions, tortures, authoritarian power and violence.

Since our last letter to Your Eminence on 26 April 2021, we have witnessed another tragic death. A committed member of the Roman Catholic faithful, **Vitold Ashurak**, 50 years old, died under unknown circumstances in the prison of Škloŭ on 21 May 2021. Over Ashurak's wounded body, his family and hundreds of people mourned his death. During the funeral in Ashurak's hometown Biarozaŭka, his parish priest, Fr Andrej Radzievich, gave witness to the dignified life of Vitold Ashurak.

He described him as a person of light who enlightened the whole community and country. Indeed, he was a local environmental activist passionate about protecting God's Creation. He was a faithful Catholic strongly committed to justice and peace. The only weapon in his hand was a rosary. His first arrest took place when he was returning home from a daily outdoor Pompeian novena prayer — launched in August 2020 in response to violence, tortures and repressions — in front of the Farny Church of the Exaltation of the Holy Cross in the city of Lida.

We are immensely glad to learn from Your letter to the Christian Vision group, that the Holy Father Pope Francis is being informed by Your Eminence about the situation in Belarus. We would like You to share with His Holiness about the servant of God Vitold and his life story, so that He can pray for his repose.

Belarus is far away from the ancient city of Rome, but there is something that connects them. In the church of **St. Martyrs Sergius and Bacchus** (Cattedrale dei Santi Sergio e Bacco degli Ucraini, Piazza della Madonna dei Monti, 3), there is an icon connecting this church to Belarus. It is known as the **Madonna del Popolo**. This fresco is a copy of the Žyrovičy jasper icon of the Holy Virgin believed to have been discovered on a wild pear tree more than half a millennium ago. In Belarus, this icon is preserved and venerated at the **Holy Dormition Orthodox monastery in Žyrovičy**.

We would like to kindly invite His Holiness to visit this icon in Rome to pray to the Mother of All and the Queen of Peace for the Belarusian people: for their suffering and dreams of the new fraternal society where peace, justice, the rule of law and solidarity prevail — as our democratic leader, **Sviatlana Tsikhanouskaya**, so well captured in her response to the Holy Father's beautiful Encyclical *Fratelli Tutti*.

We trust that with the intercession of the Mother of God, with God's grace and mercy, with our commitment to justice and dialogue made in good faith, Belarus will soon become free from tyranny, hatred and violence. We are looking forward to the day when the path for the Holy

Father's visit to our land will be open and, during his apostolic journey, he will be able to solemnly venerate the Virgin Mary in front of her precious jasper icon in the town of Žyrovičy — as the Holy See ambassador to Belarus, His Excellency Apostolic Nuncio **Archbishop Ante Jozić**, recently did in private.

In Žyrovičy Orthodox monastery, the Holy Father will also be able to see a fresco painted by another victim of the government perpetrated violence, **Raman Bandarenka**. A young artist, he was beaten to death in a courtyard of his block of flats in front of many people. The state propaganda invested heavily in discrediting Raman by insinuating his alleged alcoholic intoxication on the night of his death. Then the police destroyed the people's memorial of candles and icons at the place of Bandarenka's murder. The government attempted to silence a medical doctor, **Artiom Sarokin**, who publicly testified to 0,00‰ alcohol being found in Bandarenka's blood. Sarokin was arrested and sentenced to a prison term.

The government attempted to silence two journalists, **Katsiaryna Andreeva (Bakhvalava)** and **Darja Chultsova**, who streamed live online from a window as the police vandalised the people's memorial. They were sentenced to two years in prison. The government has also tried to silence Roman Catholic **Bishop Yuri Kasabutski**, and the Press Secretary of the Belarusian Orthodox Church, **Archpriest Sergiy Lepin**, for expressing their indignation with this act of vandalism. Both were called to the prosecutor's office and issued with a warning for extremism.

The stories of Raman and Vitold, two bright personalities who lost their lives during the ongoing political crisis in our country, have taught us that light is stronger than darkness and truth is stronger than lies. But we also have learned that human life is fragile, and if violence is not stopped soon, it produces the most tragic of consequences, ones which are irreversible in *this age*.

In the name of the Sacred Heart of Jesus, we appeal to the hearts of those in authority and power to offer hope to the suffering people of Belarus who long for freedom, justice and peace. We plead the Holy Father to intercede before Almighty God. We ask the world's leading religious body to condemn the violence and injustice from a moral standpoint. We call on the Holy See — as an important stakeholder in international relations — to use all available political instruments to help us to discover and to implement the peaceful and democratic solutions which are necessary for the effective and speedy resolution of our ongoing political crisis.

Sincerely,

Christian Vision group
of the Coordination Council,
11 June 2021 Sollemnitas
Sacratissimi Cordis Iesu

Natallia Vasilevich is a theologian, political scholar, lawyer, and moderator of the Christian Vision group. At the University of Bonn, Germany, she is currently working on a doctorate thesis about the mission of the Church in the world in the pre-conciliar process of the Holy and Great Council of the Orthodox Church (Crete, 2016).

The Vatican's Reactions to the Belarusian Crisis

Natallia Vasilevich

On matters concerning Belarus, the Vatican traditionally maintains neutrality, avoids political statements and seeks solutions to problems through diplomatic means.

Local Church leaders' reaction to the political crisis: shifting from neutrality to demands for justice

The stolen presidential elections of 9 August 2020 in Belarus were followed by peaceful protests all over the country and the extremely brutal police violence against the protestors. Thousands were detained and tortured, severely beaten and shot with flashbang grenades. Violence increased exponentially and provoked new waves of peaceful protests. On 10 August, an unarmed 43-year-old protestor, Alyaksandr Taraykouski, was shot by the police in Minsk. On 12 August, 25-year-old Alyaksandr Vikhor was detained and died without medical help.

In the midst of these tragic events, Archbishop Tadeusz Kondrusiewicz, Metropolitan of Minsk for the Catholic Church in Belarus, issued his first statement on 11 August[1]. The position of the Belarusian church leader in that document was ambiguous. Although he referred to democratic protests as 'peaceful', he insisted, however, that "the blood was shed on both sides". He called for "both parties of the conflict to stop the

---

[1] Обращение архиепископа Тадеуша Кондрусевича в связи со сложной общественно-политической ситуацией в Беларуси, 11.08.2020, https://belarus2020.churchby.info/obrashhenie-v-svyazi-so-slozhnoj-obshhestvenno-politicheskoj-situaciej/

violence". He also proposed "in order to overcome the crisis in society to urgently convene an emergency round table to decide the future of our Fatherland at it, and not at the barricades".

Such rhetoric presupposed, firstly, that peaceful protests were not so peaceful; that the protestors bore responsibility for the violence to the same extent as the police. Secondly, it sounded like a condemnation of the protests ('barricades') as a means to decide "the future of the Fatherland". This was in spite of the people's inability to change the government by the regular democratic procedure of elections, which were severely abused and rigged; in spite of the protests remaining the last resort when other means proved to be unavailable.

Kondrusiewicz's call for dialogue in the form of a 'round table' was inspired by the successful 1989 Round Table in Poland where the Catholic Church acted as a mediator between the authoritarian regime and opposition. It resulted in a peaceful transition of power and democratisation. This explains why maintaining neutrality between the two parties of the conflict was so important for Kondrusiewicz. However praiseworthy the idea of dialogue with the Catholic Church's mediation might be, it was not transferable and implementable in the context of the Belarusian crisis. The semi-condemnation of protests by Metropolitan Kondrusiewicz sounded demoralising; it was unjustifiably weak in condemning and preventing police violence.

The initial escalation of violence was stopped not by the voice of the churches and church leaders but by the chain of solidarity of Belarusian women dressed in white, holding flowers and smiling on 12 August 2020. Bishop Yury Kasabutski commented[2] on this while addressing the women of Belarus:

You took the flowers, you came out, you stood, you showed the whole world what confused everyone – in our country and in all other countries. You came out, you started waving these flowers. Your smiles, your smiles – you just amazed everyone, everyone was shocked... You came out and you began defeating evil with good...

---

[2] https://belarus2020.churchby.info/kazan-biskupa-yuryya-kasabuckaga-generalnaga-vikaryya-minska-magilyoŭskaj-arxidyyacezii-5-09-2020/

After all, if you went out and started fighting, struggling, it would not bear fruit. It has borne fruit because you came out and you overcame this evil with your goodness. You may not have known that but you defeated the devil with your goodness; the devil was also confused and did not know what to do next.

Thanks to the women's chains of solidarity, the peaceful nature of the protests became obvious and stronger. On 14 August 2020, Kondrusiewicz shifted his focus and issued an updated, more balanced and realistic statement now addressing the representatives of the state authorities in Belarus – "those in power"[3]. In this statement, the archbishop supported the protestor's claims. He insisted that the protesters were "peaceful", they were motivated by "seeking the truth about the presidential elections of 9 August", and that it is the right of the people "to know the truth which shall not be sacrificed for the sake of someone's political and opportunistic interests". He also argued, that the shed blood on the streets of our cities, the beatings of people who came to peaceful demonstrations because they wanted to know the truth, their cruel treatment and detention in inhuman conditions in prisons are a grave sin on the conscience of those who give criminal orders and commit violence.

While in his first statement Kondrusiewicz called on "both parties to the conflict to stop the violence", in the second one he addressed the authorities "to begin a constructive dialogue with society, to stop the violence and urgently release all the innocent citizens detained at the peaceful demonstrations". Moreover, on 18 August, the archbishop addressed the regime's minister of internal affairs, Yuri Karayev[4] asking him to allow pastoral visits to the detained after the presidential elections and to release all the detainees; he also asked for a meeting to discuss the ways of preventing violence in the future. On the same date, he prayed by

---

[3] Обращение архиепископа Тадеуша Кондрусевича к представителям государственной власти Республики Беларусь, 14.08.2020, https://belarus2020.churchby.info/obrashhenie-k-predstavitelyam-gosudarstvennoj-vlasti/

[4] https://belarus2020.churchby.info/arcybiskup-tadevush-kandrusevich-xocha-asabista-sustrecca-z-ministram-karaevym-kab-abmerkavac-situacyyu/

the walls of a remand prison⁵ and launched an inter-religious prayer for the resolution to the crises in Belarus⁶.

The regime's reaction to these activities of the Catholic archbishop followed soon. On 31 August 2020, he was prevented from entering the country on his way back from a private trip to Poland on the pretext of an invalid passport. Commenting on this incident Lukashenko accused Kondrusiewicz personally and the entire Catholic Church in Belarus of working against the state.⁷ At the same time, the results of the Christian Vision group's internet survey in January 2021 showed that nearly 99% of Catholics, including clergy, theologians and parish activists who mostly shared the agenda of the peaceful protests also supported Metropolitan Kondrusiewicz's address to Yuri Karayev concerning police violence.⁸

In September, following the ban on Kondrusiewicz's return to the country, the regime got instead another outspoken leader of the Roman Catholic Church in Belarus. Auxiliary Bishop Yury Kasabutski became the new voice of church leadership. In an interview on 1 September 2020, he openly condemned the persecution of the Catholic Church.⁹ On 5 September 2020, he lead an all-city Procession of the Cross in Minsk to raise awareness of these persecutions. At the event, he gave a sermon openly condemning police violence and calling for peace and praising Belarusian women protestors.¹⁰ He was often outspoken on social networks when commenting on particular cases of unacceptable violence, injustice and persecutions.

---

⁵ https://catholic.by/3/news/belarus/12038-artsyb-skup-kandrusev-ch-pamal-sya-kalya-stsen-s-za-na-valadarskaga
⁶ https://catholic.by/3/news/belarus/12031-malitva-za-belarus-pramaya-translyatsyya-z-chyrvonaga-kastsjola
⁷ https://www.interfax.ru/world/724066
⁸ https://belarus2020.churchby.info/rezultaty-narodnogo-oprosa-po-issledovaniyu-religioznogo-soobshhestva-belarusi-i-protestax-chast-3-konsolidirovannye-katoliki-i-konstruktivnye-protestanty/
⁹ https://catholic.by/3/pub/interview/12116-b-skup-yuryj-kasabutsk-spetsyyal-nym-nterv-yu-catholic-by-fakty-gavorats-shto-adbyvaetstsa-perasled-kastsjola
¹⁰ https://belarus2020.churchby.info/kazan-biskupa-yuryya-kasabuckaga-generalnaga-vikaryya-minska-magilyoўskaj-arxidyyacezii-5-09-2020/

One of those comments particularly outraged the authorities. The bishop criticised the vandalising of the people's memorial of Raman Bandarenka, a 31-year-old protestor murdered in Minsk in November 2020 by a gang of regime supporters. Lukashenko expressed his anger about the outspoken clergy of Catholic and Orthodox churches. On 18 November 2020, Bishop Kasabutski and the press secretary of the Belarusian Orthodox Church, Fr Sergy Lepin, were summoned to the prosecutor general's office. They were issued with a written warning. A week later, the investigative committee informed them of a linguistic examination of their social network posts. Even under constant control and pressure, Bishop Kasabutski continued commenting on social networks expressing solidarity with persecuted people. On 18 November, after he supported TUT.BY, the largest independent Belarusian media, unknown people attacked the building of the curia of Minsk-Mahilioŭ archdiocese.

Due to its outspoken position, the Catholic Church in Belarus, its clergy, laity, communities and organisations experienced a range of intimidation, repressions, attacks and pressure.[11]

The Vatican's reactions to the Belarusian political crisis: generic words about dialogue, rejection of violence, respect for justice and human rights

The first reactions of the Holy See to the political crisis in Belarus took place in the first days after the elections. 13 August 2020, the Holy See's Permanent Observer to the United Nations, Archbishop Ivan Jurkovič, intervened during the debate at the session of the Human Rights Council on the situation of human rights in Belarus. At the beginning of the 2000s, Jurkovič was an apostolic nuncio in Belarus. He said that the Holy See "renews its appeal for a peaceful and just resolution to the

---

[11] Natallia, Vasilevich. Persecution of the Catholic Church, Clergy and Laity in Belarus, https://belarus2020.churchby.info/persecution-of-the-catholic-church-clergy-and-laity-in-belarus/

tensions through sincere dialogue, the rejection of violence, and respect for justice and fundamental human rights"[12].

Although the Archbishop called the governing authorities to "exercise restraint and listen to the voices of their citizens and remain open to their just aspirations, assuring full respect for their civil and human rights", he, first of all, called on demonstrators to "present their requests in a peaceful way". This presumed that the peaceful character of the protests had to be the precondition for being listened to by the authorities and assigned the primary responsibility for dialogue to the protestors. The call on protestors to present their requests in a peaceful manner presumed that the protestors were doing otherwise and had to be called to peace. This wording effectively questioned the peaceful character of the Belarusian protests and, therefore, played to the regime's claims. By assigning demands first of all on protestors, by not admitting the essentially peaceful character of those protests, by putting peaceful protestors with their legitimate demands and their moral position on an equal footing with the authoritarian regime, which rigged the results of the election and had at its disposal a repressive apparatus and structures of violence, the Vatican speaker provided the regime with an indulgence for its human rights abuses and refusal to listen to the protestors' demands.

16 August 2020, after the Sunday Angelus at the St Peter's Square, Pope Francis voiced[13] his attention to "dear Belarus" in connection with "the post-electoral situation in that country." The Pope entrusted Belarus to Madonna, the Queen of Peace, and called for "dialogue, the rejection of violence, respect for justice and rights" without naming the parties responsible for the political crisis. Effectively, the Pope provided the widest possible framework for the interpretation of his views. However, taking into consideration, firstly, that the demands of the democratic movement were based on ceasing violence, re-establishing justice and the rule of law, and on a dialogue concerning the transition of power; and,

---

[12] https://www.vaticannews.va/en/vatican-city/news/2020-09/holy-see-jurkovic-un-human-rights-council-belarus.html

[13] https://www.vaticannews.va/en/pope/news/2020-08/pope-francis-prays-for-lebanon-belarus-at-sunday-angelus.html

secondly, the presence of the representatives of the Belarusian diaspora in St Peter's Square with white-red-white national flags associated with the democratic movement, and the Pope waving to them from his balcony, – the mention of Belarus at Angelus could be interpreted as rather in favour of the democratic movement.

A month later, after Archbishop Kondrusiewicz had been denied entry to the country and a special delegation from the Holy See had travelled to Minsk to resolve this matter, the Pope nuanced his statement. It was adjusted to archbishop Jurkovič's statements. At Angelus on 13 September, when the Holy See's delegation was in Belarus, Pope Frances elaborated on the situation of protest demonstrations, not naming Belarus specifically but meaning it nevertheless.[14] Firstly, he urged protestors to present their claims "peacefully, without succumbing to the temptation of aggression and violence." Secondly, he called the authorities to "listen to the voice of their citizens and welcome their just aspirations assuring complete respect for human rights and civil liberties." And thirdly, he invited churches to "do everything possible "in favour of dialogue", and "in favour of forgiveness and reconciliation".

In the case of Belarus, the protestors acted in line with the Pope's call: they presented their claims in a peaceful manner. The authorities, however, neither assured respect for human rights nor listened nor welcomed popular aspirations. In such a situation, the Pope's idea that churches should support dialogue and reconciliation was unrealistic. The two parties involved in the Belarusian crisis – the regime and the people – were not on an equal footing from the moral point of view: one side demanded dialogue, while another was avoiding it, answering peaceful and legitimate demands with repression, violence and suspension of the rule of law.

In the specific context of the Belarusian crisis, on purpose or by coincidence, the Pope's words about dialogue and reconciliation resonated with Lukashenko's proposal from 9 September voiced in his first large interview to Russian media since the beginning of the political crisis: "to

---

[14] https://www.vaticannews.va/en/pope/news/2020-09/pope-francis-manifestations-protests-angelus-appeal.html

turn the page over"[15]. While in the middle of August the idea of dialogue was promoted by the democratic forces as a means for transformation of the political regime in Belarus, in September – after the regime had started reconsolidating and unfolding the machine of repression, and the leaders of the Coordination Council of Belarus were arrested and exiled – the idea of "dialogue" and "reconciliation" sounded more like a synonym for curtailing the protest, normalising the situation on the regime's conditions and enforcing the status quo.

To an extent, that was also a semi-condemnation of Kondrusiewicz's position who, eventually, had stood up to the regime of Lukashenko and advocated for justice, human rights and suspension of violence; Kondrusiewicz grasped the meaning of the democratic protestors' claims. Despite the fact that the Archbishop's words and actions found cordial support among Catholic laity and clergy, and from the faithful of other Churches (Orthodox laypeople organised a flashmob of solidarity with Kondrusiewicz), as well as from the democratic movement making Kondrusiewicz one of its the hero-figures, the Vatican did not appreciate that. It became apparent when the "problem of Kondrusiewicz" was finally solved between the Belarusian regime and the Holy See by Kondrusiewicz's "timely" retirement.

Soon, the Vatican's appeasement of the authoritarian regime became obvious to the Belarusian diaspora in Italy too. Remembering the first Angelus in August 2020 when they were allowed to come with white-red-white flags and received a warm welcome from the Pope, Belarusian attempted to bring a large, 30 square metre, flag to the Angelus on 8 November 2020. Before coming to St Peter's Square, the group's representatives went to security to inform about the flag and its dimension. After a thorough inspection, they were told that the flag would not be allowed at St Peter's Square because it was a "Lukashenko opponents' flag", not the state flag. They were also prevented from bringing smaller flags and a banner with the word 'Belarus'. After checking their documents, the Belarusian women, including pregnant ones, were

---

[15] https://russian.rt.com/ussr/news/818401-grazhdane-belorussiya-lukashenko

asked to lift their shirts to ensure nothing was written on their bodies. This caused a great upset to the group.[16]

The next Holy See statement concerning Belarus was made following the forced landing of a Ryanair flight on 26 May 2020. The western democracies reacted rapidly and strongly by adopting on 21 June the fourth package of sanctions in response to enduring repressions and the forced landing of a Ryanair flight "to initiate a genuine and inclusive national dialogue with broader society and to avoid further repression"[17]. The Holy See's statement was announced by Matteo Bruni, director of the Holy See press office: "The Holy See is following attentively steps undertaken by different subjects which are involved in the events happening in the country. Together with this, the Vatican remains faithful to its commitment to promote democratic and peaceful solutions to the legitimate requests of the Belarusian people"[18].

This new wording was more balanced. Firstly, it included the recognition of "different subjects" in the Belarusian political process, including democratic forces, not only the regime. Secondly, a new qualification for such forces – "democratic" – appeared in the statement. Thirdly, there was an idea of the "legitimate requests of the Belarusian people" as part of the political process, which might be in conflict with the regime's interests as something opposite to the Belarusian people's interests. Finally, the Vatican positioned itself as not only an observer which "follows attentively the steps" of others but also as a contributor to solving the crisis ready to "promote" and, therefore, to be a participant in, the process.

---

[16] https://www.facebook.com/100002569450259/posts/3354393474656268/?d=n
[17] https://www.consilium.europa.eu/en/press/press-releases/2021/06/21/belarus-fourth-package-of-eu-sanctions-over-enduring-repression-and-the-forced-landing-of-a-ryanair-flight/
[18] https://www.vaticannews.va/ru/vatican-city/news/2021-06/zayavlenie-zala-pechati-o-belarusi.html

Kondrusiewicz's case: the Vatican's reaction

When the head of the Conference of Catholic Bishops of Belarus, Metropolitan of Minsk, Archbishop Tadeusz Kondrusiewicz was prevented from entering the country on 31 August, after a series of his statements against violence and in support of justice, respect to human dignity and rights, the Vatican did not produce any official statements regarding such a blatantly hostile act against the Catholic Church in Belarus. Instead, it chose diplomatic means to deal with the situation. A delegation headed by Archbishop Paul Richard Gallagher, Secretary for Relations with States of the Holy See's Secretariat of State, was sent to Minsk. Mons. Paul Butnaru became responsible for a specially established desk for Belarus in the Holy See Secretariat of State. The delegation also included Archbishop Antonio Mennini, who was apostolic nuncio in Russia at the same time as Archbishop Kondrusiewicz was leading the Catholic Church in that country; there were tensions between the two of them.

The delegation was in Minsk on 11-14 September 2020. They met with the minister of foreign affairs, Uladzimir Makei.[19] The delegation also met with Belarusian Catholic hierarchs and discussed "the way for the local Church to continue staying faithful to its identity and the Gospel mission, while also remaining an effective tool of social cohesion"[20].

Initially, this visit led not to the return of Kondrusiewicz but to the arrival of the new Apostolic Nuncio to Belarus. The office of Apostolic Nuncio was vacant, although Croatian diplomat Ante Jozić had been appointed to this position in May 2020. His episcopal ordination was still pending since 2019: initially, he was seriously injured in a car accident in Croatia, then Covid-related restrictions on mass gatherings came in place. Soon after the Holy See delegation's visit, Ante Jozić was ordained and arrived in Belarus. He became the only western diplomat to present credentials to Lukashenko as the country's president in the midst of the

---

[19] https://www.vaticannews.va/ru/vatican-city/news/2020-09/vizit-v-belarus-sekretarya-po-svyazyam-s-gosudarstvami-gallahera.html
[20] https://www.vaticannews.va/ru/vatican-city/news/2020-09/vizit-v-belarus-sekretarya-po-svyazyam-s-gosudarstvami-gallahera.html

regime's legitimacy crisis after the disputed 2020 elections, secret inauguration and continued repressions

In December, the Holy See undertook another step towards solving the Kondrusiewicz problem. The Pope's special envoy, archbishop Claudio Gugerotti, Nuncio in Belarus from 2011-2015, arrived in Minsk for a meeting with Lukashenko in the presence of Uladzimir Makei that took place on 17 December. According to Vatican press-secretary Matteo Bruni, the purpose of this meeting was "to express the Holy Father's concern about the current situation in the country"[21]. The German-language edition of the Vatican News related this visit[22] to Sviatlana Tsikhanouskaya's letter to Pope Francis in which she asked "for Your holy prayers and Your genuine word of truth and justice, which will be a blessing for all of us"[23].

However, it was Lukashenko who saw himself as a true beneficiary of that meeting: "I have always said that the current Pope Francis, from my point of view – I closely watched his predecessors, they were not bad people – but Francis is a people's man. This is what fascinates me a lot"[24].

Lukashenko was satisfied with the results of the negotiations and "considered meeting the request of the Pope of Rome possible"[25]: Kondrusiewicz would be able to return to Belarus "despite a number of negative points associated with this person", as the regime's ministry of international affairs pointed out. Lukashenko allowed archbishop Kondrusiewicz to return to Belarus on Christmas Eve. This decision was taken owing to Lukashenko's "deep respect to the Pope of Rome" and "very close, friendly, personal relations" with him.

On his return, Kondrusiewicz was not re-established as Archbishop of Minsk. Just a few days later, "The Pope of Rome Francis, a sincere person treating Belarus with love and admiration" accepted his

---

[21] https://www.vaticannews.va/de/papst/news/2020-12/belarus-vatikan-franziskus-sorge-sonderbeauftragter-lukaschenko.html
[22] https://www.vaticannews.va/de/papst/news/2020-12/belarus-vatikan-franziskus-sorge-sonderbeauftragter-lukaschenko.html
[23] https://tsikhanouskaya.org/en/events/news/f46df99254de4dd.html
[24] https://www.belta.by/president/view/lukashenko-vstretilsja-so-spetsposlannikom-papy-rimskogo-420557-2020/
[25] https://mfa.gov.by/press/statements/a1d467f90fa0d4c0.html

resignation due to reaching the retirement age on 3 January 2021, the day of Archbishop Kondrusiewicz's 75th anniversary. Bishop Kazimir Wielokosielec, almost a year elder than Kondrusiewicz, was appointed as a temporary administrator of the Minsk-Mahilioŭ Archdiocese. Wielikosielec stayed in this position until September 2021 when Józef Staniewski got appointed as a new plenipotentiary Archbishop.[26]

Belarusian experts Siarhei Ablameika and Piotr Rudkouski came to the same conclusion that, considering its capitulation to the regime and accepting the compromise, the Vatican chose the path of least resistance in the case of Kondrusiewicz.[27]

Clinking champagne glasses with the dictator: controversial nuncio Ante Jozić

On 3 November, while receiving Archbishop Ante Jozić's credentials, Lukashenko triumphantly admitted: "Belarus and the Vatican have a special relationship. In the international arena, we are consistently promoting such important initiatives as combating human trafficking, combating violence against children, protecting traditional family values."[28]

The Nuncio reaffirmed "the Holy See's support to deepening our relations. I will be open for dialogue and solving the remaining open issues for the good of the people of the country, not only of the Catholic Church, but all". Lukashenko, before joyfully clinking glasses of champagne with Archbishop Jozić, praised Pope Francis: "I respect him [the Pope] endlessly, I met many of his predecessors, but this one is the best Pope of Rome"[29].

---

[26] https://press.vatican.va/content/salastampa/it/bollettino/pubblico/2021/09/14/0570/01230.html

[27] https://belinstitute.com/be/article/adstauka-arcybiskupa-kandrusevicha-kampramis-ci-kapitulyacyya

[28] https://www.belta.by/president/view/lukashenko-prinjal-veritelnye-gramoty-apostolskogo-nuntsija-i-poslov-shesti-gosudarstv-413820-2020/

[29] http://www.ctv.by/vo-dvorce-nezavisimosti-proshla-ceremoniya-vrucheniya-veritelnyh-gramot-o-chyom-govoril-aleksandr

In the context of the persecutions of the Roman Catholic Church in Belarus and the diplomatic isolation of Lukashenko by western democracies and compared to the strong positions of the local Catholic hierarchy expressed since the beginning of the political crisis, this incident during the ceremony of presenting the Nuncio's credentials scandalised Belarusian society and Catholics.

In the Christian Vision group's internet survey, 84% of Catholics and 76% of the Catholic clergy, theologians and parish activists who took part in the survey and mainly shared the agenda of the democratic movement were disappointed by the Nuncio's behaviour during the ceremony.[30] In protest, a Roman Catholic deacon Yury Rashatko stood in front of the Minsk Archcathedral with a banner 'Contradicitur!' [objected].[31]

Another controversy related to Archbishop Jozić's acting on behalf of the Roman Catholic Church in Belarus. Although he was not its representative, he signed the appeal to Belarusians about peace and reconciliation initiated by the regime. The appeal aimed to involve religious organisations in symbolic actions in support of Lukashenko and his policies for reestablishing social cohesion, enforcing the status quo and his legitimacy as a president, and suppressing the protests.

In the pre-Christmas appeal, Belarusian religious leaders wrote: "we address our word of love with emotion to every compatriot and call for peace, forgiveness and reconciliation; we urge you to forget your grievances and continue to build our common home again and together."[32] The appeal appeared in the context of the 2021 Year of National Unity and Cohesion announced by the regime. The appeal was signed by Metropolitan Veniamin (Tupeko) on behalf of the Orthodox Church; Mufti Abu-Bekir Shabanovich – for the Muslim community; a representative of

---

[30] https://belarus2020.churchby.info/rezultaty-narodnogo-oprosa-po-issledovaniyu-religioznogo-soobshhestva-belarusi-i-protestax-chast-3-konsolidirovannye-katoliki-i-konstruktivnye-protestanty/

[31] https://t.me/christianvision/69

[32] https://belarus2020.churchby.info/religioznye-lidery-prizyvayut-zabyt-obidy-i-prodolzhit-stroit-nash-obshhij-dom/

the Chabad-Lubavitch movement rabbi Shneur Zalman Daich — for the Jewish community. In the absence of the head of the Roman Catholic Church in Belarus Metropolitan Tadeusz Kondrusiewicz, the appeal was signed not by local hierarchs, but by the apostolic nuncio Archbishop Ante Jozić.

While at the beginning of his office of the apostolic nuncio Ante Jozić's activities could be interpreted as supportive of the regime, the interest of the regime in his instrumentalisation decreased when Kazimierz Wielikosielec assumed the role of apostolic administrator in place of Tadeusz Kondrusiewicz. The role of loyal representative of the Catholic Church supportive of Lukashenko could now be played by a Belarusian bishop.

At the same time, Ante Jozić showed his care for political prisoners. On 3 June 2021, he visited Volha Zalatar, a political prisoner, Catholic volunteer and activist, mother of five children. He left a Bible and a prayer book for her. Zalatar was tortured during her arrest and detention, she was deprived of pastoral visits and religious literature. 70 Catholic priests signed an appeal to the investigative committee to end the criminal prosecution against Zalatar.[33]

During the festivities of the Bialyničy icon of the Mother of God, Ante Jozić publicly welcomed the release of 13 political prisoners in September 2021. He appealed for facilitating this process further for "the sake of the national reconciliation"[34].

Relations with the democratic forces

The Belarusian democratic movement attempted to establish its own communication with the Vatican, to draw the Pope's attention to grave violations of human rights and terror against civil society, and hostile incidents against the Roman Catholic community, expecting the Holy See to raise its voice in favour of justice.

---

[33] https://belarus2020.churchby.info/christian-vision-statement-volha-zalatar/
[34] https://catholic.by/3/news/belarus/13801-pradsta-nik-papy-frantsishka-belarusi-zaklikae-lady-paskoryts-pratses-amnistyi

Sviatlana Tsikhanouskaya, the leader of the democratic movement, was the first political leader to respond to Francis's Fratelli Tutti encyclical with an open letter, *Fraternal Society: A Vision for a New Belarus*[35], accepting the Pope's invitation to dialogue. She drew His Holiness' attention to the situation in Belarus, shared the democratic movement's vision of social and political order based on justice, love, solidarity, respect for human dignity and dialogue. Sharing the Pope's encouragement of dialogue, Tsikhanouskaya suggested it as a basis for overcoming the political crisis in Belarus. She asked the Pope:

But how should we build this dialogue? How can we demand justice if one party — the one that has weapons and power — is not going to return stolen votes or restore justice or stop violence and repression, but proposes only to "move on", "to turn the page", to accept injustice saying that it is necessary "to look to the future"? (§249)

This was Tsikhanouskaya's request to the Vatican for a more clear position, but she has never received any reply. There were other letters with similar requests which also remained unanswered. Among them: *From Francišak's Mum to Holy Father Francesco* by Volha Seviaryniec, the wife of an Orthodox believer, Christian politician and pro-life activist Paval Sieviaryniec[36]; from Belarusian political prisoners' wives and mothers[37]; from Ihar Losik, a political prisoner and Catholic believer who went on hunger strike protesting against injustice against him. In his letter, Losik appealed to Pope to raise the voice not in support of him, but in support of truth and justice in the country.[38]

Fr Viachaslau Barok, one of the most outspoken clerics of the Roman Catholic Church in Belarus and a member of the working group Christian Vision Working Group who faced persecutions for his blogging on the situation of Belarus in the light of the Catholic teaching, also

---

[35] https://belarus2020.churchby.info/sviatlana-tsikhanouskayas-letter-to-the-holy-father-francis/
[36] https://belarus2020.churchby.info/from-mum-of-francisak-to-holy-father-francesco/
[37] https://belarus2020.churchby.info/belarusian-political-prisoners-wives-and-mothers-wrote-a-letter-to-pope-francis/
[38] https://belarus2020.churchby.info/politzaklyuchennyj-igor-losik-obratilsya-k-pape-rimskomu-franczisku-s-pismom/

addressed to Pope Francis in a November 2020 video titled *Pope Francis, How Do You See Yourself in Relation to Belarus?*[39] Similarly to Sviatlana Tsikhanouskaya, Fr Barok referred to Fratelli Tutti . He asked its author, how – in the context of the parable of Good Samaritan, the central image of the encyclical – the Pope sees himself in relation to the Belarusian people:

> *The aim of my appeal is to find an answer to the question: what shall we do to bring peace to Belarus? How to stop this war?*
>
> *I have read your Encyclical, Fratelli Tutti, several times. I explained to others how relevant your message was for Belarus. However, I cannot find an answer to my own question of how it is possible to have a dialogue with those who do not want a dialogue. How the "architecture of peace" is possible without dialogue? Our Metropolitan Tadeusz Kondrusiewicz was expelled from the country as soon as he raised a question of dialogue.*
>
> *I am losing faith that those who have had a taste of human blood can come to their senses and start talking.*
>
> *At the same time, the one who proclaimed that "today is not the right time to observe laws" happily met with your envoy to Belarus, Archbishop Ante Jozić. The regime propaganda happily spread the image of the nuncio and the person who publicly confessed to ordering the murder of innocent citizens drinking champagne together. This was too much for Belarusians.*

Fr Barok received no answer from the Pope. However, two weeks later he was arrested for ten days, escorted to prison by people with machine guns and Alsatian dogs. After half a year of persecution, he became a refugee in Poland.

---

[39] https://www.youtube.com/watch?v=CajfYcdOQzg

None of the numerous addresses from the Christian Vision group received formal replies from the Vatican. The representatives of the democratic community regularly inform the Vatican about events in Belarus, about the cases of undue pressure on churches, religious leaders and laity, about violations of rights and freedoms; they report both on the most striking cases and on trends. The Vatican's contacts with the democratic movement remain mostly non-public.

The only exception was the meeting of Sviatlana Tsikhanouskaya with the apostolic nuncio in France Celestino Migliore, a former nuncio in the Russian Federation, which took place in Paris on 17 September. The possibility of Tsikhanouskaya's visit to the Vatican was discussed, however, such a visit has not happened in the end.

Also, the activities of diplomatic representatives, such as facilitating pastoral visits to political prisoners or monitoring the human rights situation in the country, are not public.

Conclusion

The Belarusian democratic movement has demonstrated high expectations and hopes for the Pope of Rome and the Vatican to raise their voices in the unequivocal condemnation of violence and injustice caused by the Belarusian regime and in solidarity with the Belarusian people. In Belarus, the image of the political orientation of the Pope and the Vatican is still under the influence of Pope John Paul II, his statements and actions in support of democratic transit in Poland at the end of the 1980s and in solidarity with the Polish democratic movement. This is the standard against which all the actions of the current Pope and the Vatican establishment are compared. Neutrality, muddy wording and visibility of good relations with the regime have led to the growing frustration and distrust.

Catholic theologians criticised such a strategy. For example, a Canada-based Irish theologian David Deane has a particular interest in this issue due to his special relations with the leader of democratic Belarus Sviatlana Tsikhanouskaya – he has known her since her teenage years. Deane appreciates the Pope's pastoral rather than political approach. He, however, insists, that "Pope Francis' acquiescence with brutal dictatorial regimes, such as Belarus, bolsters these regimes and enables their horrors". According to him, the strategy which worked for Bergoglio as an archbishop in Argentina, for the Pope it turns into an "ideological aversion to ideology", which has massive costs for people living under totalitarian regimes, like the dictatorship in Belarus, which he continues to support"[40]. Having the situation in Belarus close to his heart, Deane voices his disappointment in Pope Francis' approach, especially regarding the "deal around Archbishop Tadeusz Kondrusiewicz",[41] particularly given that the Belarusian regime "is the precise inverse of the kind of social order Fratelli Tutti calls for". Why Pope Francis has not criticized it remains incomprehensible for David Deane.

Lukashenko, on the other hand, expresses satisfaction with the Vatican's position, which he can instrumentalise to his advantage. While Sviatlana Tsikhanouskaya asks the Pope for answers, Lukashenko in his address to Pope Francis thanks him for "the achieved level of understanding, which allows finding solutions to any issues in an atmosphere of trust" and for "disinterested help and readiness for compromise which evidence that the Holy See takes care of its Belarusian faithful and is interested in strengthening society"[42].

---

[40] https://www.daviddeane.org/post/a-dictator-friendly-pope-lukashenko-and-pope-francis
[41] https://belarus2020.churchby.info/sviatlana-tsikhanouskayas-irish-childhood-friend-christians-of-belarus-are-responding-in-faith-hope-and-love-to-the-need-of-the-belarusian-people-for-freedom/
[42] https://president.gov.by/ru/events/pozdravlenie-pape-rimskomu-francisku

www.ingramcontent.com/pod-product-compliance
Lightning Source LLC
Chambersburg PA
CBHW041310110526
44590CB00028B/4311